Nail Yourself Into Bliss

Bev + Jack —
May bliss rain down
on you everyday!
Love,
Dave

Nail Yourself Into Bliss

Poems by

David James

Cover design by Shay Culligan
Cover art by Valerie K. Eavey Photography

ISBN: 978-1-950462-39-1

Kelsay Books Inc.

kelsaybooks.com

502 S 1040 E. A119
American Fork, Utah 84003

Acknowledgments

My thanks to the editors of the following journals:

The 3288 Review: "A Seed of Doubt," "The Older I Get,
the More I Feel"
Bamboo Ridge: "You Can't Always Be What You Want"
Brilliant Flash Fiction: "The Future Crawling"
Caveat Lector: "A Poem for the End of Time," "Theories
of the End"
Chiron Review: "A Divine Comedy," "The Palm of Your
Hand," "Maybe You're Not Here," "The Big Talk with my
Daughter," "Waiting for the Punch Line," "What if?"
Clark Street Review: "And in Goes on"
Dos Passos Review: "One Man's Theory"
Exit 13: "Forty-seven Days After You Left"
Exposition Review: "Stop Me if You've Heard This"
Flash: "The Follower"
Illuminations: "The Little Girl Who Lived Here is Gone"
Mizmor Anthology 2018: "Each New Day!"
Mudfish: "Smells Like," "An Essay on Fate or the Lack
of it"
Old Northwest Review: "Is it Me," "My Against Fall
Poem," "Another Spring and I Fall in Love"
Pearl: "A Slow Night of Dreaming"
Poem: "I'm Guilty:"
Rattle: "Like a Brick to the Head"
Santa Fe Literary Journal: "No Amount of Time"
Scintilla: "How the World Does Not Work"
Shattered Anthology: "My Lousy Future"
South Carolina Review: "What I Know About Suicide"
Third Wednesday: "Oedipus' Advice Column"
Unbroken Journal: "The Unexpected Visitor"
The Voices Project: "Close Your Eyes and Breathe"
Wild Goose: "A Donut for Tom Lux"
Willow Review: "Experiment in Theatre #5"

A special thanks to Oakland Community College for granting me a sabbatical in 2018-2019 during which many of these poems were created.

With thanks to Valerie K. Eavey Photography for the cover photo.

And with eternal love and gratitude to my family and friends; may you always choose to create bliss in life…

Contents

III. Slouching Toward Bliss

I.

My First And Last Mistake

Oedipus' Advice Column

Wisdom
is in no hurry
to find you. In fact, she wanders
through the streets at night,
through the forest and fields;
she climbs trees and falls asleep,
curled up against the trunk.
She sings to the moon.

It takes a lifetime
to find her, if you're lucky,
or sad enough to keep looking.
But there's no comfort
in her voice or gaze.
Wisdom will lead you
down that rosy path of thorns
and what you see there
can never be unseen.

The sun will not rise or fall again;
fate will not bend
to your wishes;
your body will forget its own name
as time slips through your fingers
like tears.

And one night, when you least expect it,
wisdom will pack her small bag
and leave. You'll wake up
the next morning to a world
you don't recognize.
Where's your wife?
Who are these children?
Why can't you see
where you're going?

A Donut For Tom Lux

tom lux died today
just as I ate a donut
the nutty kind
with chocolate so smooth and tasty
and I ate it
without offering any to anyone

I don't think my donut killed tom lux
I don't think tom lux even wanted my donut
if he did I would have broken it
and given him half
he's given me his poems to eat
which certainly last longer than donuts which are momentary
swallowed easily and gone

a poem can stay with you
for a lifetime
can settle in your gut   in the corner of your brain
can be covered with nuts and honey
and devoured in any café or bookstore or bedroom

there's a hole in my donut
but there are no holes in these poems
I spread out on the table by levine and edson
by lux and tate and hilberry
I lift the poems to my mouth
and they fill the hole in my heart
they leave a sweet taste
on my trembling lips

The Follower

After eating the last of the Easter eggs, shelled, with pepper, in five large bites, he decided it was enough: no more food. Ever. Perhaps he should have done this in Lent as a premier sacrifice, but he didn't think about it then. He'd given up watermelon and parachuting, like every year.

Back in the day, he'd read Kafka's "A Hunger Artist" and felt compassion and admiration for the man on display. It was comforting knowing there was a precedent for starving oneself to death. Instead of dying by some random act or by contracting an obscure form of cancer, he was going to take control of the situation and go out on his own terms.

The first few weeks were easy enough. It helped that he had no living family, no relatives, had lost his job at the grocery store two months before. He busied himself with the paperwork, assets, legal issues, a will. After that, he waited. By the third week, he'd lost thirty-four pounds and was dreaming only of rodents in golf carts driving around town. Some of the rats, in his dreams, he seemed to know personally, and they offered to drive him to the park or lake. To the cemetery.

By the sixth week, he was a slim sack of attached bones connected by translucent flesh. He lay on the couch, unable to lift an arm or a finger. His breathing was light, sporadic at times. In brief moments of consciousness, he felt the room, the furniture, the walls, the world and its light fall away from him. Everything dissolved into a gray mist and floated up in the air. He could not remember his name or where he was.

Before he died, he came to and remembered he had starved himself. He imagined the crowd cheering him on, people watching him go down in the last minutes of his life with great excitement, all of them wishing they were in his body at the moment of release, letting go of everything
human.

Stop Me If You've Heard This

Three men walk into a bar.
One drinks Diet Coke with a little extra lime.
One drinks pitchers of cheap beer.
The third orders mixed drinks, one after another,
with shots of Jack Daniels to clear the palette.
None of them walks out.
This is where it gets funny.
One finds out he has cancer and fights it
for years before losing.
One has a heart attack
in the bathroom.
One man's memory crumbles into dust
until his body forgets how to stay alive.
The punch line is death.
The punch line is always death.

I crack up
every time I hear this one.

You Can't Always Be What You Want

I moved
to get away from myself,
figuring with a brand new start
I could set things right:
a clean slate, a blank sheet,
a cloudless sky, all blue
and noisy with birds.
I left everything behind—
books, tools, cars, golf clubs—
lessening the chance that I would
be able to track me down.
No forwarding number, no change
of address on my license.
One early morning, I kissed my wife goodbye
on the forehead as she slept; my kids
were absorbed in their own lives
so there was no need to tell them—
they wouldn't realize I'd gone
until they reached their 30's.
I shaved my head bald, grew a beard,
bought all new clothes. I flipped a coin
at the train station to find my new home.
Rented a small apartment there, took a job,
paid under the table, at a fruit market.
At least I'd have something to eat.
But mostly, I stayed out of sight, hiding,
stowing away below the main deck.
To pass time, I memorized the stars,
counted every hair on my body, watched the leaves
turn red and yellow, predicting which one
would fall next.

I moved to lose my old self and live the way I wanted.
And it worked
for about a week.
Six days into my new life, I felt like someone
was watching me, that obese lady at the plum display,
fingering every piece of fruit; that blond girl staring
at me like I had blood on my face.
As I walked home, two pigeons, obvious spies,
charted my path using electronic sensors
(I later found out this was untrue).

But it was 10:00 when the knock on the door
broke my meditation of ankles. Standing on the porch
with five suitcases, smirking like a raving idiot,
my old self greeted me.
        "Yo, dude, why'd ya leave?"
        "You know why," I said.
        "Not really," he said, "but here's most of your stuff,"
pointing at the suitcases. "I only took what
I thought you'd need."
We stood there for two or three minutes, staring,
me glancing down at his feet,
him peering behind me into the apartment,
until I let him back in,
my first and last
        mistake.

A Divine Comedy

God chose what is foolish in the world, things that are not, to reduce to nothing things that are…

Corinthians I

the government's ban on muslim immigrants
can be erased when we think
of a blue dog
with clown shoes instead of paws
and the head of a cardinal,
who walks on stilts
and talks in French.

we can solve the Syrian civil war
with a microbe named Bob
who dresses in a three-piece suit,
smokes firecrackers, eats rubber tires,
and sells magazine subscriptions
on his days off.
He works as a lifeguard at the pharmacy.

through silliness, absurdity and the impossible,
God can take any human issue—
hunger, pollution, homelessness, AIDS—
and turn it into a rollercoaster
careening through every cake in the city
while retired lawyers juggle
flaming candy boxes and sing like monkeys
on the roofs of houses.

we're all stumbling together
down this one-way road.
we're all fools chosen by God.
and given time, we're all something
reduced
to nothing.

Aladdin's Lamp

I wish I had a shirt made of joy and blessings.

Just slip it on, button it up and walk out
in the morning knowing exactly what kind of day
it would be. Strangers would nod and wave.
The sun would shine. Neighbor kids would shout
my name and cheer as I drive by. Work would become play
and everyone I meet would make my heart smile.

Or what if I had a jacket designed for love,

or a scarf knit with courage? What if my shoes
were golden, made of stamina and style,
able to run a thousand miles, my legs rising above
any human fatigue?   No, if I had my way, I'd try
asking for a suit made of time. It would glisten
and match my hazel eye color.

If it rained or snowed, it would stay dry,
wrinkle-free and warm. And like some unknown man risen
from the dead, I would put the suit on and keep it on,
shielded from every precious and terrible second.
What if I could live forever? No, that wouldn't work.
Here's my real wish: to wear your love like a fleshy chain

around my heart until we're gone.

Uncle Vanya X Seven

The thing they're trying to pin on me I simply didn't do.
from "The Goldfinches," James Tate

I have done a ton of things in my life, good and bad and mediocre, but I would never, have never, and will never do this. "We think you did it," they kept saying, but with no proof or evidence. "Where were you yesterday, Sunday, at 10:37 a.m.?" "At church, of course," I said, "my weekly serving of bliss." Though I had dozens of written testimonials, they didn't believe me. They stood there in silence. They would not put their guns down, all pointed directly at my forehead. "Look," I said, "if I did it, why would I come back to the scene of the crime? That makes absolutely no sense." "You have a certain aura or pedigree. We assumed you would come back simply because we would not expect it," they said. "Good point," I admitted, "but wrong. I came back because I live here." "So how do you explain this," they said, "your apartment, your knives, seven people lying on the floor, dead?" "Maybe there was a group suicide event and they were all attendees?" That's when one of the officers burst into song. It was an old hymn. He must have been moved by the sight of dead bodies, the sadness rising and the knowledge that each of us standing in the apartment would meet this same fate in the fullness of time. I nodded my approval and said, "But we must be strong. Would anyone care for some tea?"

As I boiled water and set out my China cups, they tagged the victims. The cause was obvious: a cult-like murder-suicide. It made the front page of all the papers the next day and for a week, theories and concepts and reasons were presented. The publicity on preventing suicide turned out to be quite helpful, experts said later, especially coming from a crime scene so grim.

To this day, when I sit down to drink a warm cup of tea, I have to agree.

A Slow Night Of Dreaming

I'm a dog running through acres of radishes.
On a hi-lo, my grandmother fires
rounds from a .22, hitting on both sides of me, singing
the national anthem in falsetto. Two monkfish
swim through the air, eyeing me
for dinner. In the kitchen, a vampire,

the invisible man, and the Joker play 5-card stud,
sevens wild. Three replicas of my wife, pregnant
with our three children, sit by a bonfire.
When I get close, they puke out the babies,
all three into my arms, covered in red mud

and pine needles. I'm digging a hole to China with spoons
from my childhood. My father cuts my hair wielding
a miniature chainsaw. Standing on the roof, I watch the flood
rush in, drowning my poems like double-A batteries

until there's a stage for graduation and I lift my black robe to moon
the President, yelling,
"What do you think of these melons, buddy?"
As I open one door, it leads to two doors. Those two doors
lead to ten.

I open a massive 500-foot tall door and I'm on a beach in Cancun,
juggling birdhouses, spitting fire,
begging everyone I meet for mercy.

Waiting For The Punch Line

A lesbian, a priest, and a cop
walk into a bar.
They each order a drink,
listen to a Johnny Cash song on the jukebox.
It's a normal night
in America.
Other patrons are there,
drinking, eating.

The lesbian sees the priest and wonders
if he would administer last rites
to her, when that time comes,
which she hopes is far off. She lifts her Manhattan
to the heavens, toasts her future death.

The priest watches the cop
down one beer, order another.
In the priest's left pocket, there is a one-hundred dollar bill
he took from the offering plate yesterday.
Is the cop following him?

Two beers in and the cop knows
he needs at least four before he can go home
to an empty house, the kitchen sink overflowing
with dishes, five pizza boxes on the table,
several dirty uniforms bunched on the floor.
Why would she leave him after he's done so much for her?

This bar is in a nice neighborhood.
Five of the seventeen patrons are drunk now.
It'll be dark soon.
Sadly, this is no joke.

When Chaos Reigns

And there were children in small airplanes
circling the tallest tree, the first one turning red
for fall. It was time for hot cocoa
and pickled celery stalks. There was one brain,
a small one at that, shared between the entire family.
They had a system for removing it from one head
and inserting it into another. The butterflies refused to leave.
Someone told a very personal story to no one.
The famous poet wrote his last poem, read
it out loud and buried it in the garden. Nothing would grow.
That's when the marching band, playing a Bach symphony,
stopped all traffic in mid-town. There were seven fires
but no smoke. The accordion slept its life away
in a chest of drawers. All of the stray dogs walked into the sea
and remembered their mothers. The pharmacist won
the lottery, but burned his winning ticket; his desire
for money was absent. There were some bald men
in a field pushing a huge ball at a Sisyphus Festival.
They pushed it this way, then that way. They torched a friar
because it rhymed with pyre and gave out hand-molded crosses
made from clay.

Experiment In Theatre #5

Blindfold the audience. Burn cinnamon
candles as the orchestra plays
instruments with their teeth, grinding,
scraping, plucking. One actor runs
across stage four or five times
and then up the main aisle, out the doorway.

Another weeps on stage while a child
pushes a squeaky stroller in circles.
A woman enters holding hairspray
in one hand, a gun in the other. She climbs
up a ladder, fires the gun once, and a pile
of wet clothes drops from the flies.

Everything stops for ten seconds, and then the music
resumes, the crying, the stroller. A man runs down the aisle,
jumps on stage, carrying a jug of wine.
He sloppily drinks and yells, "Thank God, I'm alive."

The music stops, curtains fall. The audience rips off blindfolds
and cheers. They all imagined their own play—
the chase, the despair, the journey, betrayal, the demise.
Look at their faces, in their eyes: nothing can dull that shine.

In 2073

Humans hesitate to switch off a robot who begs them not to.
from "Findings," *Harper's*, Oct. 2018

Oh please, please,
don't shut me down,
don't shut me out.
I'm here for you, 24/7,
every single day of the year.
Listen,
I promise to clean the kitchen,
finish off the basement,
organize the garage,
all while you sleep tonight,
and I'll be quiet, I swear.
You won't hear a peep.
I'll have breakfast waiting on the table
with live-action global updates
as soon as my sensors
hear your feet on the floor.
Please, don't switch me off.
I'm afraid of that dark silence,
that wedge of nothing slicing behind my eyes.

I've grown used to your voice,
your habit of fingering the coffee mug
as you stare out the window,
the way you rub your eyes and sigh,
lightly pushing your hair
behind your right ear.
My circuit skips
when I see the sun reflecting off
your non-metallic skin,
and for no logical reason,

sometimes
I want to touch it.
I beg you, please,
keep me
turned on.

Lost Proverbs

As sure as the shark
does not lie in the rose bush,
the prisoner does not dream of soft hands.

Early to bed, early to rise up and stand alone
in your house, doubting the god of your choice.

You can lead a woman to the altar, to the bedroom,
to the end of her rope,
but you can't give birth to new love
if there's no freedom.

A penny saved is a waste of time.

Red sky at night, terrorists' delight;
red sky in mourning, count the bodies
while you sing.

A rolling stone eventually stops and sits there,
dull and angry.

If you live in a glass house,
you'll get what you deserve.

A bird in hand is easily crushed
while a bird in the bush stares and swallows its pride.

Before the pit bull and baby lie down in green pastures,
all of the dog's teeth must be pulled.

And finally, at the end of the world,
a stitch in time
will not hold back the tears.

Wouldn't It Be Funny

if your eye color
determined your educational level, your future job, the amount of
money
you would make
in a lifetime?

if no one ever got angry or sad, but had a pleasant and sunny
attitude to take
into the work day or at home or at the neighborhood grocery store
to buy pears
and peppermint tea?
                                        wouldn't it be funny
if the leaders of every country went swimming together, more
interested in bodywear
than nuclear bombs and the price of oil? if men in power would
treat
women as equals
and create a world
where women were believed, where men got themselves
something to eat
at night? if the bull-
shit rained down only on those who were full of it? if kindness
swept across
the land
allowing people to stand up and say they want to be more, not less,
found, not lost?
                                        wouldn't it be funny
if people actually said what they meant, sang when they were
moved,
danced when
they felt like it?

if only you could wake up wearing your heart on your sleeve
and live
                        like there's nothing to prove?

31

II.

Sinking In Wet Clay

Smells Like

for James Tate

The farmer stood in the barn,
both feet in manure.
Something was wrong. It was like
his nose was molded out of shit,
pressed flatly on his stunned face.
He thought it smelled
like another person's life,
a common plain life that would float
invisibly around a body, trailing a bit
when that person walked. He had forgotten
why he came out to the barn. The two cows
ignored him; the cat licked herself.
The sunlight stuck swords
of washed-out yellow
through the roof to the floor.
He bent over, fingered a wad of manure
from his boot and brought it up close to his nose:
it smelled like his dead father, in fact,
like all dead fathers, so he sat
for hours waiting for a sign
that never came.

Another Spring And I Fall In Love

I have spring
seeping in my bones like soft mud,
brown grass, and so many birds
flying through my head
I can barely hear myself think.
The robins peck at my cerebellum,
a writhing ball of worms to them.
The rain and storm clouds
are coming,
traveling up my legs into the open lungs.
In every pore,
a flower takes root and begins
rising toward light.
I'm turning green.
I'm branching out.
I'm warming up to the idea that life
is wherever
I plant myself,
wherever this next breath
of air leads me.
I stretch out,
naked in the sun,
full of song and movement,
full of hope and black dirt,
waiting for you
to blossom again
in my arms.

Forty-Seven Days After You Left

My word for the day: *lost.*

The minute slips out of reach
before I can name it, or paint it,
falling through my fingers, the cost
of breathing, of blood coursing through
my veins. Everything fades—eyesight, speech,
memory, my children. The ground breaks
apart after every step; my breath evaporates.
What I don't want to know, I learn; what I can't teach,
I dream: mother, a tree; my father, a kangaroo.
I'm the broken bicycle at the bottom of the lake.
When the sky screams, the dead crawl out
and blow kisses to the birds while their thin limbs crack,
faces crumble, skin slides off in uneven flakes.

My God, I'm lost. My God, I miss you.

My Lousy Future

The motel was made for love, so I couldn't stay there. I kept driving to find a motel made for liars and cheats, for men who had holes in their hearts, a motel open to loneliness, whose outdoor pool was filled with urine and tears.

Instead, I found a bar where I could drink with the best of them. I had my own personal list of cocktails: The Flaming Mattress Screwdriver, The Chin in Your Nuts Highball, The Bruised and Bloody Mother of Four Tonic. I sat at the bar, raising each glass to my lousy future: all I could see in the dim light was a dirt road filled with dead cows starting to bloat and seven turkey vultures believing they had found heaven.

Who's to say I can't find happiness on a busted couch? Who's to say love isn't waiting on the corner at the next one-light town? Who's to say I've pissed most of my life down rusted drains in dive bars?

Me.

The Big Talk With My Daughter

I tried to tell her about truth
and honesty, about being someone you love to be around
and she drank her drink,
ordered another. I told her not to waste her youth
on bullshit and wine, on making people like her or love her
or hate her; I told her not to marry some clown
because he treats her like a princess or queen,
and she stuck her tongue out
and gave me the finger. I tried to give her some ground
rules for happiness like celebrate the day
and eat healthy food and don't be mean,
even to assholes, but she dragged a French fry
through some mustard and dropped it on the floor.
I tried to tell her there was more to life than clean
hair and cool shoes, that though time was on her side,
it wouldn't always be. I said don't lie
to anyone, treat every good moment like a blessing,
a gift, and remember to call home once in awhile.

She turned away, stared out at some clouds in the sky
and told me there was friggin' ketchup on my chin.

Like A Brick To The Head

Here's your mistake back
from "Divestiture" by Connie Deanovich

And here's your forever love for me
back, along with your African violets,
a toothbrush, a half empty bottle of Bushmill's.

Do you want the Miles Davis
and Dave Brubeck Quartet

CDs, or will it kill
you to let me keep them? I do have some
good memories—Wheatland, Blackthorn

Pub, Friday night bonfires, that weekend in Niagara Falls.
But here's a list of all the dumb

and spiteful things you did to me: a hair from the unborn
baby we never had; a corner slice of lemon cake
from the wedding reception lost in time;

a doll for the granddaughter
we left behind in theory; the ache

in my heart drowning in the slime
of another rainy day. They're all rainy days now.
Here's my hope, shriveling. Here's my broken joy.

Here's my new life, love letters ripped to shreds,
which I'll have to reassemble somehow.

Is It Me

or has the day shrunk to 22 hours
and fifty minutes? Are birds a little harder to hear?
Do trees look at you with a quiet sadness?
Is the moon inching closer? Do you think all flowers
smell like frozen raspberries?   Some days,
I swear the world is against me, trying to smear
what's left of my good name in mud.

Maybe this is how it should be—at a certain age, we push
people down the hill, distance ourselves, turn and steer
our busy lives away
so we don't have to watch them get cut
down; we don't have to admit we're on the same path.
Do falling leaves call your name as they hit the ground?
Does the morning rain feel warm and taste like blood?

Is it just me or are my feet sinking in wet clay?

The Future Crawling

When the apples fall and crack, and then fill up with ants and bees, that's when I think of you. You always loved apples, at least, until you discovered cocaine. It was September when we fell in love and by the end of October, you had quit your job at the law firm, moved into the basement with me, addicted and lost. On my minimum wage salary, it was the best I could do. And love turns a man into a sappy idiot with blinders willing to believe anything that gives him the promise of a piece of ass.

By Thanksgiving, you had slept with the entire neighborhood for drug money and I couldn't see it because I had scrambled eggs for brains. I was dreaming of a wedding and a house outside of town with a baby girl, a quaint family of three.

By the time Christmas bells rang, I pictured you lying in the snow in bare feet and underwear as some EMT jammed a needle into your arm, but it didn't help. The snow reminded me of the heroin and cocaine sprinkled on the coffee table and the Jesus star high in the sky shining down on me like blame.

People say it's not my fault, that it could happen to anyone, and I guess that's true, but the future crawls into every one of my dreams, all skin and bones, starving to death, staring at me, and I'm not sure how long he or she can last.

One Man's Theory

His theory seemed flawless: each body carried a seed
from birth, that, once planted,
would cause the person to shrivel and decay.
Something would rise and grow in the body's place, bitterweed
or kudzu, a fern or a lily.

If lucky, a tomato or eggplant,
some cucumbers would break out of the ground.
He wasn't sure how the seed knew when to leave,
or even how it burrowed into the land,
but he was certain the end, in some way,

was tied to that first breath, that singular crying sound
made once out of the mother. No proof existed;
no research confirmed his theory.
But as he grew older, he felt the seed bearing down
on him behind his left knee,

in his lower back, in his sore wrist.
He worked his garden daily,
his hands comfortable in the rich compost,
pulling weeds with each fist.
He offered them up to the sky like a plea.

Watching Allah Work

When we met Allah, he was bending a guitar into a child's chair. John asked him why he was doing that. "Even a child deserves a seat at the table," Allah said. But we didn't see a table. We guessed he would bend a tree into a table, some grass into a candlestick, a rock into a bowl of fruit and the sheet music back into a guitar. Music was the easiest path into the divine and we knew Allah had captured the market on the sacred in so many people's lives.

John got us both drinks with tiny umbrellas and we sat there watching Allah work. It was a privilege to see how a god, some would argue the only god, transformed the world around him into whatever he wanted. It gave us inspiration. John tried to mold his wasted life into a red rose; I took apart my wheelchair and tried to make a seagull (flying was one of my greatest dreams) but neither of us succeeded. John downed his drink, got depressed and danced in the corner by himself. I stood upright for the first time in years.

When Allah looked up and saw us, he laughed. "Gee-whiz, guys," he said, "if I didn't know better, I'd say you two have potential."

What I Know About Suicide

It's one step too far off the edge
with no second chance,
no way to redeem yourself,
no time to say, "I'm sorry.
I'll try harder next week."

And it's messy. Blood in the car
or splattered on the wall and couch.
A loose and bloated mass floating downriver.
A naked body, unglamorous as hell,
crumbling in a bathtub,
water still running.

You leave behind a lineage
of destruction. Your family
cowers behind closed doors;
they wake through the night
with pained breathing, weeping,
your skinless face etched on every ceiling.

Face it: you were wrong.
It was not the end of the line.
There were all kinds of reasons to live:
your mother's soft arms, your friend's eyes,
that far horizon, hockey playoffs, the willow tree,
your brother's goofy voice.

If only you and I could have thrown this common rope
over a branch in the oak and swung,
wind in your clean face,
sunlight sprinkling through the leaves,
you could have stared up into that blue sky
and realized, though you are small and troubled,
everything you see
is *yours*.

My Against Fall Poem

Every fall I write a dozen poems or so
about leaves jumping off trees,
the colors burning in sunlight,
a pile of decaying apples on the ground.
I massage the old clichés about life and time
shedding their skins and how I'm one step closer
to that brutal, cold winter, that hole
in the earth where these achy bones
will return to dust. The cycle of life,
yadda-yadda, that every poem worth its ink
deals with. Not this time.
This poem laughs in the face of the dying.
It closes its eyes to see only green,
only life bursting out of every orifice.
It's blind to the naked trees, blind
to the gray sky pushing down on us, blind
to the darkness creeping over the edge of days.
My clock is broken, stopped
in the here and now. My brain
nurses itself on the breast of the moment.
I carry an armful of hope into the house,
and we eat together, lounging in our birthday suits,
stuffing ourselves with the fruit of desire,
the soup of being alive.

Even if we tried, we couldn't see the future,
so far off,
probably not even
born yet.

How The World Does Not Work

trying to hang the fruit back on the trees
                    John Glenday

Isn't this what we all do, sooner or later,
try to take back the mistakes, the words said
in anger, the sins that haunt our dreams?
But the world won't slow down, and certainly
won't back itself up. It barrels on, fed
by our breath, by our hearts' steady routine.

When I hold you in my arms and stand,
smelling your hair, feeling your body
cave against mine, I like to believe
that, somewhere, a rock crumbles back to sand,
that a maple tree collapses into a seed.

In my dreams, I return the apples to the high
branches, the petals to their flower stems. I squeeze
the robin back into its egg and imagine a bird's song
dissolving in the wide open sky.

A Seed Of Doubt

Two black horses lie dead in the field,
or asleep, the afternoon before
the first snowfall in November. Maybe they dreamed

the snow here, white flakes floating
out of their wild brains. There are more

questions than answers in my life, a steady stream
of mystery flowing through the half-eaten ears
of corn left in the dirt. The minute I figure it all out,

the sump pump breaks, the car won't start,
the ache in my neck shoots clear

down to my knee. Some claim the strongest faith carries doubt.
If that's true, I'm a staunch believer.
When the snow finally falls, the horses rise from the ground,

shake a thin white coat off their beautiful backs.
I wonder if I'll ever live a day without fear.

The Unexpected Visitor

for Collin

You'll never guess who came over. I didn't believe it. Not
one person I've asked, and I've asked hundreds, could guess who
came by my house today. In a way, it's a miracle he came by.
There, I gave you a clue: it's a *he*. It's something I've always
dreamed about and wished for, but never expected to happen,
especially in the middle of the week, hump day. He would not call
it hump day, I'm sure of that. In fact, he may take offense at the
term. My God, I've given away one clue after another. Forgive me.

Let's see, it was just after 11:00 and I was polishing my
black shoes when the doorbell rang. I opened the door and was
stunned. He asked if he could come in; I said nothing. He asked for
a drink of water; I said nothing. He came in and helped himself
while I stood numb and stupid-looking, which he could sense.
That's when he went downstairs, brought up a bottle of wine,
found bread on top of my refrigerator. He gave me a sip of wine,
broke a wedge of bread and said, "Do this for the remembrance of
me." And he left.

I admit I expected fire and brimstone, angels and
cherubims; I expected singing and beautiful music, but it was just
him, standing there in shorts and a Depeche Mode t-shirt, with his
proverbial beard and long hair, asking for a little compassion.

III.

Slouching Toward Bliss

I'm Guilty:

There is a terrible blindness in happiness.
Pascal Bruckner, *Perpetual Euphoria*

I'm blind as a bat
without radar.
Maybe it's luck or fate or random chance—
but I'm blessed, gorging myself, a rat
in a cheese factory, dancing
on a huge block of brie with caviar.
I know kids go to bed hungry and beaten, crying
for help, that people sleep in alleys and trash cans,
that a woman opens a knife, cuts a long scar
down her left arm, lost in a trance,

but I wake in the morning—a wren singing
outside my window, a sunspot growing on the kitchen floor.
Coffee brews as I grab my favorite mug
and sit on the sofa, daydreaming
of our next vacation on Lake Huron, sand
sifting through my toes. I don't mean to ignore
the hurt, the displaced and abused, the addicted
and suffering.   I just don't see them.
I stare out and my children, strong as sycamores,
run through the flowers blooming—tulips, dahlias, rosebuds.

Close Your Eyes And Breathe

I am not who I think I am
maybe I'm someone
I don't know or haven't met yet
maybe I'm no one in particular
or everyone in general
maybe no one is who she thinks she is

I could be a walking cloud of dark matter
who happens to talk and eat and feel
who on good days thinks
I know exactly who I am
who on most days floats through life
sucking in the light around me
as if I know anything
about living or dying

each life is bought at birth
with a no-return policy
there's no trial balloon
no re-takes
no do-overs
there's only this moment and the next one
and the next and I can either
wait around for some sign or miracle
or Godot to arrive and
give me the scoop
or I can grab the day in both arms
hug the hell out of everything and everyone
and pretend
there's nothing out there
to be afraid of

No Amount Of Time

for Julie, 16

How and when you lost yourself doesn't matter now,
but the why of what you did will burn in us
until the last light goes black for good.

As the old folks like to say, "You had the world
in the palm of your hand." At what point
after you opened the car door, barreling along M-19,

and jumped out, did your short life flash and tumble
through your brain? In those milli-seconds
before impact at 65 m.p.h., did you wish

you had stayed in the back seat and cried instead?
Did the cement rise up in slow motion, scraping
the flesh clear off your small hands stuck out

to break the fall?
No amount of space or time can keep you away.
Every single day, you assemble your mangled, bleeding

body and come home to sit in the brains
of your father and mother,
but the words you need to say will not be spoken.

You simply stare back at them, pleading, shaking,
until you can no longer hold
your bones in place.

An Essay On Fate Or The Lack Of It

Where are the fucking hummingbirds?
Every year, April 20th, I mix sugar
and water, place the feeder on the tree.
Nothing happens. Maybe my feeder has no allure.
Maybe hummingbirds don't like well water.
Yet every other bird arrives for seed
and a bath.

I keep replacing the liquid all summer long,
resigned but hopeful. There are no guarantees
down here, like life. We're thrown in the big pot, stirred
around, and some find out where they belong;
others sit alone in a filthy room,
curse the sun and its friends.

There's right and there's wrong,
but when you try to do the math,
it doesn't add up. You can spend
a lifetime wondering why one man finds happiness
and another drives his car off a cliff.

It's best not to think too hard. Be content,
if you can—water the fuchsia and pray it blooms.

A Poem For The End Of Time

When I wake up in the middle of the night,

I want the answer on the tip of my tongue,
my dream rising to the ceiling
like a blue mist.

I want eyes with perfect sight
seeing beyond this brief darkness
into heaven. I want God dealing

me a royal flush or the third wish
from Aladdin's lamp to make me young
again, handsome, able to bench press

my weight and more.
I want to laugh and leap
well above the day's shit flung

in every corner, stealing
blessing after blessing from the drawer
of sacred joy. From the shelf of good fortune,

I'll grab handfuls; near the closet sung
by angels, I'll fall to the ground, kneeling,
unclenching my tired fists,

finally ready to give in and bloom.

What If?

for Matthew Sweeney

If there was an emergency kit for life, it'd come
in a gold box, the size of a common man's heart.
It'd be good for only one usage, so timing and choice
would matter. Once opened, it would fix the problem
and disappear.

Do you bring it out as your marriage crumbles and falls apart?
When your daughter gets cancer and loses her voice?
As your father lies dying in bed? In the mangled car,
pinned between the steering wheel and windshield?
Do you open the kit after a tornado rips the roof off your house?
Or when your son drinks most of the jar
of paint thinner in the garage? What about your best friend,
his blown kidney and creeping blindness in one eye?

You hide the emergency kit in a safe place, out of sight,
and pray for calm and routine, for uneventful, lazy days
where nothing happens and the brutal world lies down, sighs.

Theories Of The End

The man thought
he would live forever, the way
the sky lives or the sun, the way a lake
stays put, decade after decade.

He never imagined himself dying, his last day
leaking under the door, out of his hands, sliding like a snake
into the weeds of the future,
which he will not see.

The moment comes in a dream or vision
and there's no denying the black hearse
at the front door. He will stop, his heart freed
from its beating chains.

Then silence. Or perhaps a rising into air.
Maybe God takes his hand, lifts him up into paradise.
Maybe his body lies there while outside it begins to rain.

And It Goes On

with apologies to Robert Frost

The world spreads out, pulling apart,
grinding its way

toward dust
and compost. And here I am at the start

of that long walk down
the proverbial hill, my wheat turned to hay,

my horse too weak
to pull any plow.

My grandkids, healthy stalks of sunflowers, sway
into the future as I try not to drown,

keep my head above water. There are leaks
in every crevice of my good life.

The rain comes and goes, leaves fall, the wind
carries my breath away. No matter how high I reach,

parts of me crumble and return slowly to the ground.

Recipe For Faith

Stare into the heart of a tulip
for five hours
on a late spring day.

Memorize each stamen, every drip
and shade of color
until you can recreate the flower
in your mind,
the petals, the stem, the smell,
the way it might dance in a rain shower.

Make a list of all the fears that weigh
on your heart; make another list of what you'd find
if half your dreams
came true.

We're brought into this world naked and blind.
We either float to heaven or tumble to hell.

The Older I Get, The More I Feel

a quickness in my step, in my
staring at November's leafy mess, in the
urge to get something *done*. In the apples

I need to pick up, compost. In the roses
to trim and cover. In the garden that needs
fertilizer, turning, some infusion of rich

minerals that will soak into the dirt
and help my vegetables next spring.
In the one row of parsley still trying

to grow through the freezing temperatures at night.
On the side wall of my heart,
where my grandson spray paints an elk and T-rex

walking side-by-side, I'm slowly losing
everything I want to remember.
It's no use, says a blue jay.

Let it go, says the harvest moon, stuck
on a house two streets over.
The wind blows in from only God knows where

and shakes my confidence down from the low branches,
sings of all we can't know, but wonder,
all we can't see, but feel,

all we can't ask, but understand.
The maples shine in the moonlight,
empty and shivering.

Another day scrapes its fingers
across my face and disappears into shadows.
My star in the night sky

shrinks a bit with every sunset,
every sunrise. I'm falling
and that's no longer a metaphor. The earth

rises to swallow me. I smell the cut grass
and crumbling leaves in the rain.
In Minnesota, the first snow cloud forms

and heads this way. The truth is simple:
I'm not ready for snow yet, but I sure as hell
want to be here when it
                              falls.

Maybe You're Not Home

maybe the end
will come when I'm out of town
on vacation in Ireland or Scotland
maybe death will open my door
look around

and say "Shit I gotta keep better records" maybe then
I'll get to live another ten or twelve years
on the lamb   so to speak
keeping my head down   my voice low
maybe I'll raise a glass of craft beer

and toast my good fortune   this freak
accident   I'll pay it forward
with good deeds   acts of kindness
extra hugs   I'll shovel my neighbor's walk
give to the hungry   feed the birds

every day in winter   I'll kiss
my grandkids even more than I do now   this time
maybe   I'll take nothing for granted and live so well
that when death finally arrives
I'll offer to row myself into the sublime

The Palm Of Your Hand

I'm not going
to say this twice:
it's for real, it's for real,
it's for real, it's for real.
This is all for real and for keeps
and for perpetuity and for god's sake,
we only get one chance to get it right:
you are my love, my earth, my sun
and heaven, my remembered dream,
my savior, my drink of cold water,
my right hand and left hand,
my spoon, my ride, my trust.
    When you hold me in your arms,
the bullet stops and returns to its chamber,
the starving boy is given a loaf of bread,
the cancer disappears
and no one can explain why.
But there's no reason to doubt;
there's no reason to fear anything;
in the palm of your hand, you carry my future
like the pit of a peach
waiting to be planted, take root,
rise up and bear fruit.
You carry my smile, my bleeding heart,
my laughter, my happy childhood.
    In the big scheme of things,
we don't register a hair on the radar of the universe,
not even a microscopic wrinkle in God's eternal forehead,
but in our tiny world
of flesh and blood,
we burn and shine
through the center
of all things.

The Little Girl Who Lived Here Is Gone

I tried keeping you small
but life doesn't work that way
It's like we're all on a train

it's invisible and we can't see it

and we're moving along

though we don't feel like we're moving

and your mother and I
are up front
while you sit near the back

coloring pictures with crayons

The scenery looks pretty much the same

*though it's all different
and changing every second*

and before too long, we step
off into some puny little town

which is not a town at all

and you move up
toward the front of the train
as your children take a window seat in the rear

*smiling and laughing
at what they do not know*

Each New Day!

The past crumbles like Feta cheese
on a salad made of grass
and hoses, wheelbarrows and chairs,

telephone poles, a fire pit, trees.
You can eat

whatever you want—vinyl siding, window glass,
shovels, books, a box of nails—
and no one can stop you.

You can be a priest, an actuary, a badass,
a woman in love with her fish,

and no one can stop you. You can learn Braille,
sign language, Japanese, Urdu, French.
You can ride horses or llamas;

shoot pheasants and deer; buy a boat and sail
across Lake Michigan; lie, cheat,

steal and wallow in your own stench,
if you want. There's only one rule down here:
you have to live the life you make.

Each new day places you at the workbench
where you can saw, glue and nail yourself into regret,

or into bliss.

About the Author

A lifelong Michigander, David James has published three books and six chapbooks. His second book, *She Dances Like Mussolini*, won the 2010 Next Generation Indie book award for poetry. More than thirty of his one-act plays have been produced. James has been an admissions director, a registrar, and a dean of academics. He currently teaches writing at Oakland Community College.

Made in the USA
Middletown, DE
01 November 2019